It's Raining Cats and Dogs

It's Raining Cats and Dogs

All Kinds of Weather, and Why We Have It

by Franklyn M. Branley

Illustrated by True Kelley

Houghton Mifflin Company

Boston

Library of Congress Cataloging-in-Publication Data

Branley, Franklyn Mansfield, 1915–
   It's raining cats and dogs.

   Bibliography: p.
   Includes index.
   Summary: Discusses various weather phenomena,
including rain, hail, smog, snow, lightning,
hurricanes, and tornadoes.
   1. Rain and rainfall—Juvenile literature.
   2. Weather—Juvenile literature. [1. Weather]
   I. Kelley, True, ill. II. Title. III. Title:
It is raining cats and dogs.
QC924.7.B698   1987   551.5   86–27546
ISBN 0-395-33070-X

Printed in the United States of America

A   10 9 8 7 6 5 4 3

For Margaret—F.M.B.
For Jada, lover of clouds—T.K.

Contents

It's Raining Cats and Dogs

1. It's Raining Cats and Dogs — And Worms and Frogs and a Human Hailstone

When there's a heavy storm, people sometimes say, "It's raining cats and dogs." In 1969, Hurricane Camille dumped 27 inches of rain on Gulfport, Mississippi. On one day in 1972, almost 74 inches of rain fell on the island of La Reunion in the Indian Ocean. If anyone could say it was raining cats and dogs, it would be people in those places.

The saying may go back to Odin, an ancient god of northern Europe. Often in pictures of Odin, wind is shown blowing from the heads of the dogs and wolves with him.

The behavior of cats is often thought to be caused by the weather. They may seem nervous before a storm. British sailors say, "The cat has a gale of wind in its tail."

Perhaps the saying "It's raining cats and dogs" comes from weather beliefs like these. Or it may have come from a Pennsylvania German saying: "It's raining cats and ducks." People said rain was good for cats because they could stay inside and sleep by the fire. And it was good for ducks because there would be plenty of puddles for them.

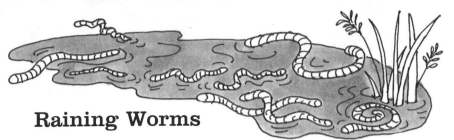

Raining Worms

No one has ever reported seeing cats and dogs falling out of the sky, but some people think it rains worms. After a heavy rain, there are often lots of worms on sidewalks and roads — so many you might think it had rained worms. But it didn't. What happens is that when a lot of rain falls so fast that the water cannot drain away, it fills in the worm holes. The worms crawl to the surface of the ground to keep from drowning.

Falling Frogs

In Dubuque, Iowa, on June 16, 1882, frogs really did fall from the sky during a hailstorm.

When it hails there are heavy storm clouds that may tower eight miles high. Strong winds blow up and down inside the clouds. Water droplets freeze, and the ice pellets may get very large before they fall from the cloud. The hailstones at Dubuque were up to five inches across, and small frogs were found inside some of them.

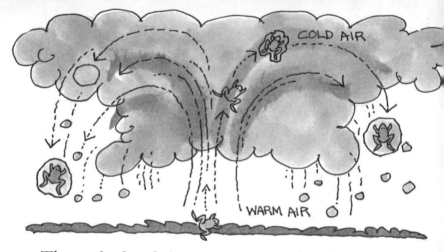

The updrafts of air were so strong that they picked up the tiny frogs and carried them into the storm clouds. There it was so cold that droplets froze on them. The frogs became encased inside layer upon layer of ice.

A Human Hailstone

In 1930 sixteen German glider pilots were flying in a contest to see who could reach the highest altitude. They flew into storm clouds that were building over the mountains. Powerful winds carried them upward before they realized their danger. Fourteen of the pilots managed to get their planes out of the updraft and out of the thundercloud. But two of them were trapped. They were swirled up to 30,000 and 40,000 feet. The fierce currents broke up their gliders and the pilots had to bail out. One of them parachuted to earth safely. The other pilot was carried up and dropped inside the cloud. Layers of ice froze on him. He fell seven miles to his death — a human hailstone!

July 15: St. Swithin's Day

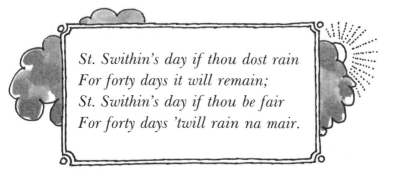

*St. Swithin's day if thou dost rain
For forty days it will remain;
St. Swithin's day if thou be fair
For forty days 'twill rain na mair.*

St. Swithin, who died in A.D. 862, was later made the patron saint of Winchester Cathedral in England. According to some historians, he asked that he be buried outside the church, and he was. On July 15, 971, however, his remains were moved into the church, and, as soon as this was done, miracles began to happen. It seemed that, to protest the moving of his remains, St. Swithin caused a deluge that lasted 40 days — convincing the monks to have second thoughts about the whole idea. And so the legend was started.

Maybe so. No one knows for sure, nor do we know why the belief has lasted so many centuries, especially since the weather it foretells never happens. Imagine the results if there were 40 days of rain, or 40 days without a drop!

However, you can check for yourself. See if rainy weather follows a wet July 15 or if a drought follows a dry one.

Cloudbursts

When you suddenly break a balloon full of water, the water gushes out of it. That's what happens in a thunderstorm. Air moving upward keeps the water from falling. The water builds up until there is so much it can no longer be held in the cloud. The cloud "bursts" and great amounts of water fall, causing flash floods in valleys and canyons. Rivers may suddenly rise ten or twenty feet. Streams at the base of canyons may flood, even though it's not raining there. A wall of water from the mountainside may move down a valley, turning over cars and rolling them downstream. It may roll heavy boulders, tear out trees, destroy buildings and bridges.

Wettest and Driest Places on Earth

Each year some 26,000 cubic miles of water (200 billion gallons) fall on land around the world. Most of the water comes from evaporation of seas and oceans. The map shows where the most and least rain falls.

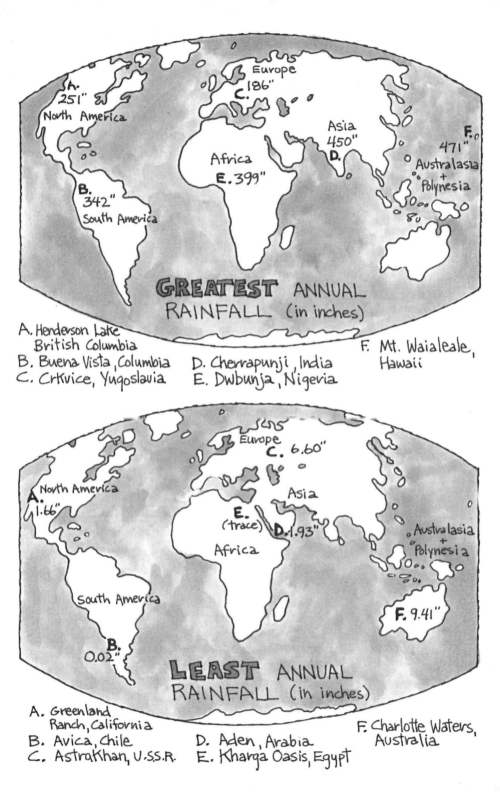

GREATEST ANNUAL RAINFALL (in inches)

Europe 186"
Asia 450"
Africa E. 399"
F. 471" Australasia + Polynesia
A. 251" North America
B. 342" South America

A. Henderson Lake British Columbia
B. Buena Vista, Columbia
C. Crkvice, Yugoslavia
D. Cherrapunji, India
E. Dwbunja, Nigeria
F. Mt. Waialeale, Hawaii

LEAST ANNUAL RAINFALL (in inches)

Europe C. 6.60"
Asia
E. (trace) D. 1.93"
Africa
Australasia + Polynesia
A. 1.66" North America
South America
B. 0.02"
F. 9.41"

A. Greenland Ranch, California
B. Avica, Chile
C. Astrakhan, U.S.S.R.
D. Aden, Arabia
E. Kharga Oasis, Egypt
F. Charlotte Waters, Australia

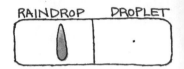
Millions of Raindrops

Rain comes from clouds, which are made of droplets of water so small there are a million of them in a single raindrop. A tablespoon could hold 7 billion droplets. Raindrops are much larger. They may measure a quarter of an inch across, though more often they are smaller, perhaps only one or two hundredths of an inch across.

When air is still, the droplets fall at a speed of about 6 miles an hour.

Seeing the Size of Raindrops

You can see the size of raindrops when they first splash on a dry sidewalk, or you can catch them on a piece of cardboard. Here is another way to see the size of raindrops:

PUT ABOUT ¼" OF FLOUR IN A PIE PAN OR SAUCER AND SMOOTH.
THEN COVER THE DISH AND TAKE IT OUTSIDE.
REMOVE THE COVER FOR TWO OR THREE SECONDS... (NO LONGER, BECAUSE MORE THAN ONE DROP MAY FALL IN THE SAME PLACE.)

There will be lumps of flour where the raindrops fell. Let them dry for an hour or so, or bake the drops in a very low oven.

8

PUT THE FLOUR THROUGH A SIEVE TO SEPARATE THE LUMPS. THE BIGGER THE LUMPS, THE BIGGER THE RAINDROPS.

Try this when the rain is gentle and again when it is heavy. Try it at the start of a storm and after it has rained for a while.

Here's another way to measure the size of drops. This time you'll use a coffee can.

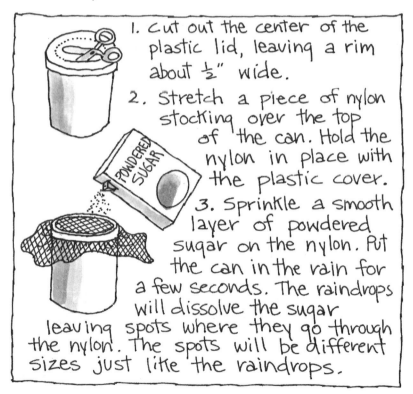

1. Cut out the center of the plastic lid, leaving a rim about ½" wide.

2. Stretch a piece of nylon stocking over the top of the can. Hold the nylon in place with the plastic cover.

3. Sprinkle a smooth layer of powdered sugar on the nylon. Put the can in the rain for a few seconds. The raindrops will dissolve the sugar leaving spots where they go through the nylon. The spots will be different sizes just like the raindrops.

9

What Shape Is a Raindrop?

Raindrops are shaped like hamburger buns. As they pass through the air they are flattened and look something like this:

Inside a spaceship, where there is zero gravity, they would look like this:

How Much Rain?

How much rain falls during a shower, or during a day, week, or month? You can find out by measuring it.

Put an empty coffee can or any straight-sided container where rain can fall into it. Place the can away from any trees, bushes, or buildings.

When it stops raining, put a ruler in the can so the ruler touches the bottom and read the level of the water.

Suppose it measures one inch deep. (That would be a lot. More likely the water will be only one-quarter of an inch deep, or even less.)

Keep a record of the rain that falls.

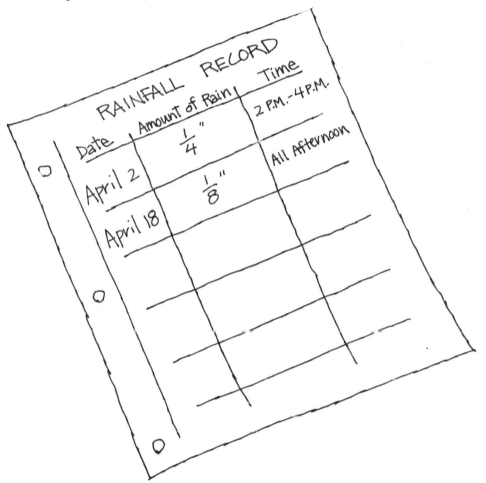

RAINFALL RECORD

Date	Amount of Rain	Time
April 2	$\frac{1}{4}$"	2 P.M.-4 P.M.
April 18	$\frac{1}{8}$"	All Afternoon

An Accurate Rain Gauge

Using a coffee can gives a rough indication of small amounts of rainfall, but it cannot be accurate because it's hard to measure the water with a ruler. You can make a more exact gauge, one that measures in millimeters.

11

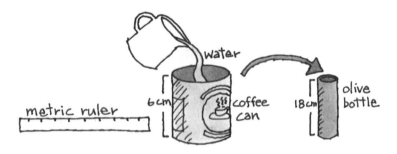

metric ruler · water · 6cm · coffee can · 18cm · olive bottle

You will need a metric measuring stick and two containers: a coffee can and a narrow, straight-sided glass container such as a bottle for olives. Pour six centimeters (60 millimeters) of water into the can. Then pour this water into the bottle. Fasten a piece of masking tape, or another tape you can mark, vertically to the outside of the jar. Let's say the water column in the jar is 18 centimeters high. Therefore six centimeters of rainfall in the can measures 18 centimeters on the gauge. (The ratio is one to three: one centimeter in the can equals three centimeters in the bottle.) Mark the center of the tape three centimeters, the top of it six centimeters. The first three centimeters on the gauge equal one centimeter of rain in the can; the second three centimeters (the six-centimeter mark) equal two centimeters in the can, and so on.

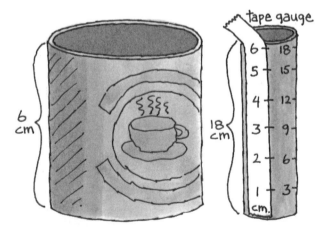

tape gauge

6 cm

18 cm

6 | 18
5 | 15
4 | 12
3 | 9
2 | 6
1 | 3
cm.

1 cm. of rain in the can equals 3 cm. in the bottle. This makes it easier to make accurate readings of small amounts of rainfall.

When it rains, place the large container outside. Pour the rain you collect into the bottle and read the level of the water. This will give a fairly accurate measurement of the amount of rain that has fallen.

If six centimeters of water in the can overfills the bottle, work backward to mark your gauge. Fill the bottle and then pour the water into the can. Suppose there were 50 millimeters of water in the bottle and when poured into the can the depth was five millimeters. Then one millimeter of rainfall would equal ten millimeters on your gauge.

50 mm = | 5 mm   THEN I mm = 10 mm on the gauge.

How Much Rain Falls on Your School Yard?

Suppose rain falls steadily for several hours, and your rain gauge shows that three centimeters of rain fell during that time. That means 30 000 cubic centimeters fell on each square meter of the ground; that's 30 000 grams, or 30 kilograms.

1 meter = 100 centimeters
1 square meter = 100 × 100 (10 000 square centimeters)
10 000 × 3 (cm of rain) = 30 000 cubic centimeters

A cubic centimeter of water weighs close to one gram, so 30 000 cubic centimeters weighs 30 000 grams.

If you know the area of the lot your house or apartment is on, or of your farm or your school yard, you can figure out how many tons of water fall on it during a storm.

Suppose the area of your school yard is 70 by 100 meters (about 200 by 300 feet), or 7 000 square meters. If 30 kilograms fell on each square meter, then 210 000 kilograms fell on the school yard — that's 210 metric tons. (An inch of rain falling on one acre, 43,560 square feet, would be 27,143 gallons, or 113 tons of water.) A storm frequently spreads over towns, counties, and even states, so billions of tons of water would fall during that single storm.

Greatest Recorded Rainfalls

In one day: 73.62 inches (more than 6 feet) on La Reunion, a small island in the Indian Ocean, March 15, 1952 (equal to 8,327 tons on each acre)

In one month: 366 inches in Assam, India, in July 1981

In one year: 1,041 inches in Assam, India, from August 1860 to August 1861

Rainmakers

In times of drought Indians used to have rain dances, and many tribes still do. The traditional belief is that if they dance long enough and hard enough, the gods will bring rain. Sometimes it works.

You don't have to dance to make rain. You can make it in your kitchen with a glass pot, a saucer, and some ice cubes. Here's how:

Put a cup of water in a glass saucepan or coffee pot. Cover the pot with a saucer filled with ice cubes. Warm the water a little and keep it over low heat.

ice cubes on saucer

1 cup water

low heat

After a while you'll see droplets on the bottom of the saucer. Warm air and water vapor in the pot cool when they meet the saucer. The air cannot then hold the water vapor, which changes to tiny droplets.

Clouds in the sky form in the same way. If you continued to heat the water, the droplets would become bigger and then they'd fall, just as raindrops do.

In early days rainmakers banged on drums and made smoky fires, trying to coax water out of the clouds. They also exploded bombs in the air, hoping to jar the rain loose.

As far back as 1890 patents were issued for rainmaking devices. One of them released pellets of dry ice, which is frozen carbon dioxide, into the air where it would mix with water droplets. The droplets would grow on the small bits of dry ice, becoming larger and falling to Earth. The plan was a good one, but there was no way to get the dry ice into the high clouds. This kind of rainmaking was first done successfully in 1946, using an airplane. The droplets did join together, and there was rain. Since that time rainmaking has become quite common in many western states.

One early rainmaker of 1880 used a kite to carry an explosive into a cloud. Once there, an electric charge set off the explosive. It's doubtful if this idea ever worked.

Today, smoke containing silver iodide crystals is also used. The smoke is sent into the air from earth-based fires or from airplanes that fly through the clouds. Dry ice "snow" is also used. The silver iodide crystals and the pellets of dry ice are "seeds" on which water droplets grow and combine to make raindrops.

When conditions are just right, with heavy clouds and cool temperatures, seeding often produces rain. But the method is far from effective. If it works in one out of five attempts, that is a good record.

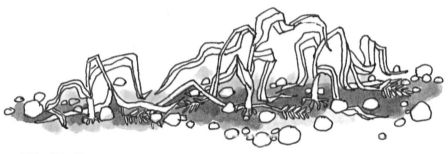

Hail Stoppers

When there is severe drought, rain making is called for. But when there is severe rain (or hail), hail stoppers are needed. Hailstones (chunks of ice), sometimes as big as golf balls, can flatten crops and do a lot of damage to buildings. People have tried to stop hail from falling, or at least to reduce the size of the hailstones.

In 1896 Albert Stiger, an Austrian, designed a hail-stopping cannon. It was aimed straight up and enclosed in a tall chimney that directed the sound waves of the explosion skyward. Dozens of these cannons

THE
STIGER
HAIL STOPPING
CANNON

were set up. When they were first tried, in 1897, they were successful, and no hail fell in the area. The idea spread to Italy, where there were also good results. Although hail was not eliminated there, the hailstones were smaller, and so the storms caused less damage. Very likely the explosions speeded up freezing, and caused hail to fall before additional layers formed on the hailstones.

More recently, rockets have been shot into storm clouds and exploded, although the results have not been especially good. Cloud seeding has also been tried. Russian scientists say that they have been 80 per cent successful in reducing the size of hailstones by seeding storm clouds with dry-ice pellets.

Control of Rain Making and Hail Stopping

In a typical year, 1977, clouds were seeded in 88 rain-making projects in the United States. That included 23 states and 7 per cent of the land area. Most of these efforts were not coordinated, however, for there is no single agency responsible for them. Many farmers complained that rainmakers take their rain away when rain is made to fall on land other than their own.

By seeding and other weather-control activities it should be possible to increase winter snowfall, increase rainfall in farm states, and reduce damage from hurricanes, tornadoes, and hailstorms. Also, it should become possible to poke holes in the clouds, letting the sun shine through.

Most people feel the weather changes should be made, for they could save crops and prevent many disasters. But effects on areas other than the one in which rain falls or in which the storms occur must be studied. Weather management must serve all the people, not a select few. Perhaps those who do cloud seeding should be licensed, and their activities should be cleared by a central office.

Sea gull, sea gull,
Sit on the sand.
It's sign of a rain
When you are at hand.

Before a rainstorm, there is often a drop in the density of air and the air is less able to support a bird. Since it's harder for them to fly, the gulls are more apt to stay on land.

Rain before seven,
Clear by eleven.

Probably true: rain may be caused by a rain belt which often takes four hours or so to pass by.

When ants travel in a straight line,
 expect rain;
When they scatter,
 expect fair weather.

It's highly unlikely that ants behave in this way before a rainfall. However, don't take our word for it. Watch ants to see if there are any changes in their behavior that you can relate to the weather. The connection here may be more valid than in another old legend that says, "Step on an ant, and it will soon rain."

2. We Make Our Own Weather

Rain making isn't the only way people change the weather. Some weather changes are not planned; they happen because many people live in cities. As cities grow, forests are cut down and fields are covered with pavement, roads, and buildings. This causes changes in the weather, for example, in temperature.

Because of the concentration of people, factories, cars, and air traffic in cities, temperatures are usually higher than in the suburbs. This is because:

1. heat is trapped in narrow streets between tall buildings;

2. there are many people, and they give off heat;

3. chimneys give off heat in winter; and

4. cars give off heat and gases that hang over the city like a blanket, holding in city heat.

City Winds

Because cities have high and low buildings, narrow and wide streets, winds are broken up. Wind speed is less in a city than in the countryside, but there is a lot of turbulence; winds are strong in one place and weak in another close by. They may blow fast along a street and then cause strong eddies or back flows where streets cross. Turning a corner, a person might walk from a calm into a full gale. Scraps of paper, dust, and dirt may suddenly be blown up along the walls of some buildings, or downwards on the sides away from the wind.

How to Test Turbulence

This experiment shows how the flat surfaces and sharp corners of buildings cause turbulence.

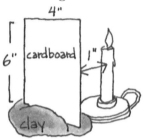

Place the narrow edge of a four-by-six-inch piece of cardboard in some modeling clay, or use spring clothespins to hold it upright. Set a candle about an inch behind the cardboard. When you blow on the front of the cardboard, the flame will bend toward the back of it. (You can see this if someone else blows on the cardboard. Be careful to keep the flame away from the cardboard.) The card produces a turbulent flow, the way a building does when the wind blows on it.

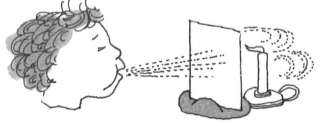

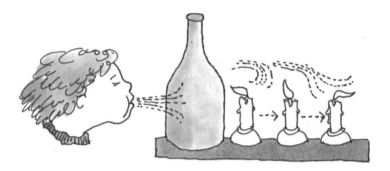

Even rounded buildings cause turbulence, as you can see by replacing the cardboard with a bottle. When you blow on the near side of the bottle, the flame will bend toward it. If you move the candle away from the bottle, the turbulence will decrease. If you keep moving the candle back, you will reach a point at which the flame will finally blow away from the bottle.

Dirty Air in the City

The air over a city usually contains more solid particles than does the air over the suburbs. Eventually the particles fall out. In large cities such as Detroit and Chicago, 700 tons of dust and ash fall on a square mile every year.

The particles filter sunlight, removing much of the ultraviolet part — the part that causes a person to tan. City workers don't get out into the sun much; but even when they do, they receive little ultraviolet light. That's one reason why city workers are palefaces.

But the pollution in city air causes more serious problems. One of these is smog, a mixture of fog, smoke, and other chemicals. Some fogs develop over

cities because factories and electric generators put tremendous amounts of hot water vapor into the air. When the air is calm, the vapor condenses at low levels and produces smog when combined with the sulfur dioxide given off by factories and the nitrous oxides given off by cars. These compounds become sulfuric acid and nitric acid, which are very harmful when breathed into the lungs. The acids also eat away stone statues and buildings, and they corrode metals.

In 1978 smog caused a series of accidents involving 100 cars on a Los Angeles freeway. In 1952, 4,000 people died from a heavy smog that shrouded London. In 1965 smog overlaid Donora, Pennsylvania. It killed 20 people and sickened thousands more.

Testing for Air Pollution

The pollutants in air are often gases that we cannot see, but we can see the corrosion they cause and the destruction of lakes and forests caused by acid rain. If there are particles, they are often very small and so cannot be seen any better than gases can. But we may be able to feel them.

You can try collecting solid particles that may be in the air. Mix some plain gelatin, following directions on the package. Put just a thin layer of the gelatin on several saucers. Place these saucers at various locations and leave them for a day or so. When you collect the saucers, be careful to label them so you know where they were placed.

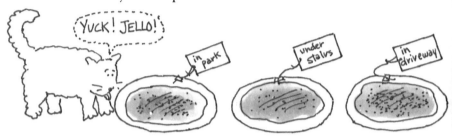

With your eyes alone you may see dust particles that have stuck to the gelatin. If you use a magnifying glass or a microscope you may see a lot more, for often the particles in the air are very small.

Perhaps you'll find very few particles, and that would be good. On the other hand, you may find that some of the places were pretty dusty.

City Smog

Pollutants from houses, factories, incinerators, cars, planes, and ships may collect in the air and hang over the city, often not going away because of what is called an *inversion*. Usually air temperature decreases with altitude; the warmest air is closest to the ground and tends to move upward. But sometimes the situation is

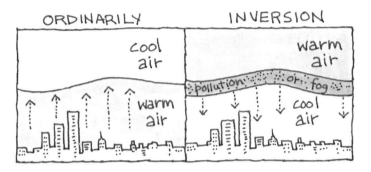

ORDINARILY

cool
air

warm
air

INVERSION

warm
air

Pollution or fog

cool
air

inverted — turned upside down. A layer of cooler air hugs the ground, and warm air lies above it. This warm-air layer acts as a blanket, so the pollution gases and particles are trapped and held over the city.

An inversion may trap fog over a city. During the day, fog may develop in the region surrounding the city. Since the city is somewhat warmer it may remain free of the fog. Then at night the fog may drift into the city, moving downward and hugging the buildings. The next day, particles of ash and dust above the city may reflect sunlight away, preventing the heating and evaporation of the fog. So the fog may hang over the city long after it has disappeared from the countryside.

The most dangerous gases that become trapped in the air over a city are sulfur, from the burning of oil and coal, and nitrous oxides, from the exhausts of gasoline and diesel engines.

Large amounts of sulfur are given off when soft coal is burned. Hundreds of thousands of homes and offices in London used to burn soft coal. Sulfur and ash mixed with the fog that formed along the Thames River to make the "pea-soupers" of London — dense fogs that contained so much sulfur that people had trouble breathing. Soft-coal burning has been outlawed in London, and so conditions are much improved. Even so, it is estimated that every year 6 million tons of sulfur from the burning of oil and hard coal go into the skies over London. In New York more than one million tons of sulfur go into the air, plus two million tons of carbon monoxide (a deadly poison) from car and truck exhaust.

There are ways to reduce the amount of pollution. Although there are more cars than ever, new cars are required to have built-in devices that reduce the amount of oxides they give off. Even so, fogs containing oxides, which become smogs when they combine with smoke, still form above many cities. A classic example is Los Angeles, which has one of the world's heaviest concentrations of cars and which often is covered with a layer of heavy smog.

To decrease fog formation, and also reduce the particles in city air, factories now have taller chimneys. The gases that go up the chimneys are hot, causing them to rise rapidly. The hot gases and ash from the factories are picked up by the winds that often blow at higher elevations and are carried hundreds of miles downwind. For the city, the problem is solved. But for other areas, new problems are caused. Ash and gases in the upper air combine with water to produce acids. Factories in midwestern states have been largely responsible for producing acid rains that have caused so much destruction of lakes and forests in northeastern states and in Canada.

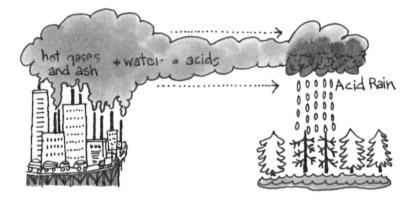

3. Pink Snow and Green Snow — And a Blizzard on the Fourth of July

On July 4, 1918, the world was at war, and Americans wanted to make that July Fourth unforgettable. On the Great Plains — Wyoming, Montana, Idaho, the Dakotas, and parts of Colorado and Utah — towns had parades, speeches, and barbecues. The morning activities everywhere went off well.

Just as the people were finishing their feasts, the sun disappeared behind heavy clouds, and a cold wind swept across the plains. Temperatures dropped rapidly; rain started to fall. People scrambled for cover. As they did, the rain turned to hail. Then it was snowing — and what a snow it was! The wind howled, and the snow was blown into drifts. This was the Great Blizzard of 1918.

The railroad telegraph sent word that the blizzard covered many states, and it looked as though it would go on snowing for a long time. People were warned to take shelter. Towns were crowded with visitors, but all were cared for in the homes of the townspeople. Stoves were started up, blankets were spread on floors, food was brought from cold storage in the cellars.

Hour after hour the storm howled and blew. Three days later the sun finally came out. People began to clear the snow away. Visitors plowed through drifts and struggled back to their houses.

This was truly an unforgettable year — 1918, the year it snowed on the Fourth of July and kept snowing for three days.

Pink Snow and Green Snow

Everyone knows that snow is white — or is it? Sometimes people in western states and Canada see snowfalls that are pink or green. The pink snow is caused by small bits of reddish soil that are carried into the air. The particles are like tiny grains of talcum powder, light enough to float in the upper air. When it snows, the particles cling to the snowflakes and are carried to the ground. Instead of ground covered with a blanket of white snow, the countryside has a pinkish glow.

Another cause of colored snow is plankton. Tiny plants, so small that you need a microscope to see them, live in the ocean. They are called planktons. There are also kinds of plankton that live in the upper air. They are called frost plants, or cryoplanktons. (*Cryo* means low temperature.) The cryoplanktons are single-celled plants and animals that live in snow and ice. Certain of these very small frost plants show a pink or a greenish color. When it snows, masses of them may be collected together by the falling flakes. Billions and billions of them contained in the snow give the countryside a soft glow of pink or green.

The speech bubble reads: 49,999,999,999,999,561

How Many Flakes in a Snowstorm?

It seems impossible to count the flakes in a snowstorm. But a college professor did it, and this is how.

In 1978 Boston, Massachusetts, had a snowstorm that paralyzed the city for days. The average depth of the snow was 27 inches. A local radio station had a contest to find out how many flakes there were. The professor found the area of Boston — 43 square miles. He multiplied this by 27 inches. Then he divided the answer by the volume of an average snowflake — the space it occupies. This is 1/10,000 of a cubic inch. (There are 10,000 flakes in a cubic inch of snow.)

Here's the answer. The number of snowflakes that fell on Boston was 50 quadrillion, in mathematical shorthand, 5×10^{16} — 50,000,000,000,000,000 snowflakes.

How Much Water in the Snow?

Some places have snow all winter. It stays on the ground until spring when it begins to melt. Sometimes there is too much water for streams to carry. That's when there are spring floods.

How much water is there in snow? It's easy to find out. All you need is a coffee can and a ruler. Before it snows, put the coffee can outside. It should stand up straight, and be placed away from trees and buildings.

When it stops snowing, measure the depth of the snow with a ruler. Be sure the ruler touches the bottom of the can.

Bring the can inside and let the snow melt. Then see how deep the water is.

If there are five inches of snow in the can you'll probably have about half an inch of water.

SNOW   MELTED

People often say that a foot of snow equals an inch of water. That's not always true. Sometimes snow is light and dry; it would take more than a foot to equal an inch of water. At other times the snow is wet and heavy. Less than a foot would equal an inch of water.

Dry snow is made of small crystals that usually fall over regions far from the sea. It can blow between cracks and crevices. Dry snow is great for skiers, because it does not melt and clog the skis.

Wet snow usually falls in coastal regions and is perfect for packing into snowballs or snowmen (or snowwomen). Dry snow can be handled by snow blowers, but wet snow clogs them and so must be removed with plows.

Catching Snow

If you live inland from the sea you may have storms of dry snow made of small, light flakes. Hold a piece of black cloth outside during a storm and catch a few flakes — just a few so each flake is separate. Look at them through a magnifying glass. You'll have to do this outside, otherwise they will melt. You may see that each flake is in the form of a six-sided crystal. And no two are alike.

William Bentley, an American farmer, got interested in snowflakes. During his lifetime (1865 to 1931) he photographed flakes under a microscope. He had a collection of 6,000 pictures, and each snowflake was different.

Light snowflakes form when water vapor freezes — a direct change from a gas to a solid. Because of the way water molecules are put together, the crystals that form are always six-sided.

If the snow is wet, chances are you won't see these crystals. Separate flakes most likely will have melted together. There will also not be crystals if the snow is more like sleet, because sleet is often a mixture of snow and frozen rain.

Snow Keeps Things Warm

That's hard to believe. But you can prove it with this experiment. You must be in a cold, cold place where the snow is at least a foot deep.

Put a thermometer outdoors. Leave it for ten or fifteen minutes and see how far down the temperature goes. When it stops, record it.

Now dig a hole in the snow all the way down to the ground. Put the thermometer in the hole. (First put it in a plastic bag.) Then fill the hole with loose snow.

After ten or fifteen minutes, uncover the thermom-

eter. It will probably be warmer than it was in the air. It will surely be warmer if the day is windy.

In order for snow to be a good insulator, it must be light. That is, there must be a lot of air between the snowflakes, for it is the air that prevents the loss of heat.

Many farmers say, "A year of snow is a year of plenty," and there is considerable truth in that. When the ground is cold and bare, plants suffer from wind and freezing rain. Under a blanket of snow, they are protected. Deep snow also provides a supply of water for new plantings in the spring. Snow is called the poor man's fertilizer, because it contains small amounts of the many substances that are suspended in the air before a snowstorm. The more snow, the more nitrates and other minerals there are available for crops to feed upon.

SOME RECORD SNOWFALLS IN THE U.S.

In one storm	Mt. Shasta, California	189"	Feb. 13-19 1959
In one day	Silver Lake, Colorado	76"	April 1921
In one month	Tamarack, California	390"	February 1972
In one season	* Paradise Ranger Station, California	1224"	1971-1972

* Average snowfall at the station is 575 inches, or 48 feet!

1977 — The Year of the Great Snow

In 1977 the western part of the country had little snow. But the northeastern states had a lot more than they wanted.

In January 60 people died in blizzards, and there was a dangerous shortage of fuel oil because trucks could not get through the deep drifts.

Buffalo, New York, had a total of 16 feet by the end of February. Boonville, a bit north of Buffalo, had 23 feet. Drifts of snow were 30 feet deep, higher than houses and telephone poles. The snow packed so hard that plows could not go through without choppers.

There was so much snow cities had no place to put it. In Buffalo thousands of tons of ice-hard snow were loaded onto freight trains. They took it out into vacant areas where it could be dumped.

Farmers and ski resorts like to have snow — it protects crops and grasslands and, of course, it brings people to the ski runs. But in 1977 there was a lot more snow than anyone wanted. The snow was a disaster, and so also were the floods that occurred when the snow melted.

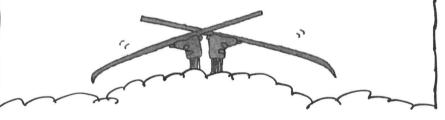

4. Lightning Never Strikes Twice?

Don't you believe it.

During a single storm, the Empire State Building in New York and the Sears Tower in Chicago may pick up several lightning strokes.

And there are people who have been struck many times, often with most unusual results.

Hit Seven Times by Lightning

Ray Sullivan is a retired national park ranger. During his lifetime he has been struck by lightning seven times. He has been knocked out. His hair has been burned off, his hearing has been damaged, a toenail has been torn off, and he has been picked up and thrown into the air. One time his watch was melted. And every time he has been struck, some part of his clothing has been burned.

No one knows why Ray Sullivan should have been hit so often. But he is not trying to find out. He has a lightning rod at each corner of his trailer home and in the six trees close by. If lightning strikes, it will most likely hit one of the rods and be carried into the ground where it can't hit anyone. Even so, whenever there's a storm Ray Sullivan goes into his bedroom and sits scared until it is over.

Cured by Lightning?

In 1971 Edwin E. Robinson, a truck driver in Falmouth, Maine, became blind and partly deaf as a result of a car accident.

Nine years later, on June 4, 1980, during a thunderstorm, he heard a sound like a whip cracking above his head as lightning crashed in on him. It knocked him over and he was unconscious for several minutes. Somehow he got to his bedroom, where his wife found him later in the day. Excitedly he exclaimed, "I can see you! I can see again!" Also, in the next few weeks hair started to grow on his bald head.

The wires inside his hearing aid were burned out, but he no longer needed it. He could hear again.

Did lightning cause a "miracle" cure? Perhaps, but some physicians find it hard to accept that lightning could restore vision and hearing — and make hair grow. His eye doctor said that nothing had been wrong with Mr. Robinson's eyes. The blindness had been caused by damage to the brain. But the doctor could not explain why sight had returned. Some people suggest that Mr. Robinson's troubles may have been emotional and that the lightning startled him enough to change his attitude. Whatever the explanation, Mr. Robinson is one person who was lucky when he was struck by lightning.

Ways That Lightning Causes Damage

Vaporization: Lightning causes water to change suddenly to vapor, and so it expands. Vaporization of the water inside a tree may cause the tree to explode. Vaporization of the water in the structure of the pavement or a highway may cause it to heave or shatter. Rocks may explode when water in crevices expands rapidly.

Melting: Nails in buildings may be melted by lightning. Sand on a beach may be melted into glassy clumps. There is a record of a man in England who was struck by lightning. He had a metal knee joint, and when he was struck the joint welded together without serious injury to the man.

Burning: This is the single most costly effect of lightning. More people are killed by lightning than by any other weather phenomenon, and by far the largest number of them are killed by lightning-caused fires.

Conduction: Lightning may be carried along overhead wires. The wires can lead the lightning to generating stations, into transformers on poles, or into buildings. It can explode a television set, knock out a fuse box, or follow a telephone line to the telephone receiver.

Pressure changes: Near a lightning strike, the air may be compressed, knocking down people and even buildings. Or, the air pressure may drop suddenly. A person's clothes have been ripped off by the sudden pressure drop.

Direct strikes: A person alone in an empty field makes an excellent target for lightning. It may go right through the person from head to toe. It may kill the person. Or, miraculously, it may cause no damage.

Make Your Own Lightning

Lightning is a discharge of electricity. You can make a spark that is very much like lightning, though much smaller. You've probably already done it many times.

Scuff across the carpet on a cool, dry day. Then touch your finger to a doorknob. There will be a snap as a spark jumps to the knob. You were charged with electricity. When you touched the knob, you discharged. You were charged with about one hundred volts; a lightning discharge is made of millions of volts, and it's very hot — hotter than the sun.

You can make an electric charge holder out of a bottle. You'll need a bottle with a cork or a plastic top. Cut a piece of wire from a coat hanger. (A piece of copper wire will work even better.)

plastic cap

1. Push the wire through the cap and bend it as shown. (Be sure the bent part is small enough to go through the mouth of the bottle.)

2. Cut a strip of light aluminum foil about 2" long and ¼" wide. Bend the foil and hang it on the wire.

3. Carefully put the foil and the wire inside the bottle.

4. Tear up a piece of paper into small scraps.

5. Rub a comb on a wool sweater or on the carpet. Bring the comb close to the small scraps of paper. If the comb is charged, it will pick up the scraps.

6. Rub the comb again to make sure it has a good charge. Touch the comb to the wire. The ends of the foil strip will stand apart. They are charged.

Touch your finger to the wire, and the foil strips will collapse. The electricity went from the foil to your body.

Lightning is the same thing — static electricity. The charge is built up when particles in the air rub together and when drops of water in the air break into smaller droplets.

How Much Electricity Is There in Lightning?

Amounts of electricity are expressed in amperes, and the pressure of electricity is expressed in volts. When multiplied together, the result is in watts:

$$volts \times amperes = watts$$

A lightning discharge may be as high as 200,000 amperes, though some have been known to go as high as 350,000 amperes. A discharge may be as great as 15 million volts, so the wattage is tremendous. Discharges last only a few millionths of a second, however, so there is small chance of trapping and using their energy.

Heat Lightning

On a hot summer evening, broad expanses of the sky may be lighted even though there is no thunder or rain. People often call this heat lightning, because it seems different from ordinary lightning.

Actually the brightening of the sky is caused by a distant storm. The storm may be so far away that streaks of lightning cannot be seen and thunder cannot be heard.

St. Elmo's Fire

St. Elmo is the patron saint of sailors. His "fire" is a glow that often appears at the tips of the masts and yards of sailing ships during a lightning storm. This glow is produced when the ship becomes charged with electricity, and the electricity discharges at the tips of objects. The effect may also be seen on lightning rods, steeples, tree branches, and the tops of chimneys.

Ball Lightning and Will-o'-the-Wisps

If you ever see a bright ball of light moving about, get a camera quickly and snap it. Your picture will be the only one of its kind, because there is no proven photograph of ball lightning.

Not all people agree that ball lightning exists. Certainly those who believe they have seen it are convinced that it does. It is usually reported as a glowing ball with fuzzy edges, and somewhere between 4 and 12 inches across. The ball may be stationary or it may move along a metal conductor such as a window frame. It may go through a window or even a solid door.

In 1940 an English gardener reported that on a clear day he saw at his feet a blue-green ball about two feet across. It seemed to be made of "strings" of light in motion. After about three seconds, it rose, went over trees and houses, traveled about a quarter of a mile, and landed. There was a loud explosion, and a building near where it landed was damaged.

There are many similar reports. Some people say it is nothing more than an image left on the eye after a lightning flash. Because of the uncertainty about ball lightning, it is credited with all sorts of effects. Some people believe that it kills any person or animal it touches, smashes objects, boils water in kettles or pails, and disappears usually with a loud explosion.

What people call ball lightning may actually be will-o'-the-wisps. These fleeting "flames" that may appear over swampy places are believed to be glowing methane or swamp gas, a product of the decay of vegetation. The gas makes strange, luminous shapes that flicker across the countryside and fade into the night.

Lightning Rods

You may have seen steel rods on the trunks of large trees or rods that rise higher than the tops of the buildings they are fastened to. These are lightning rods that go from the top of the structure to deep under the ground.

Lightning follows the easiest path. So, if lightning strikes a tree or building with a lightning rod it will be carried harmlessly into the ground by the rod.

Television antennas may serve as lightning rods. In addition to the antenna wire that goes to the set, there is another wire that goes from the supporting rod to the ground. If this ground wire isn't large enough to carry the charge, the lightning will follow the wire to the television set where it can cause a lot of damage.

Inside a Thundercloud

Thunderclouds, or thunderheads, tower upward on a hot summer day, sometimes as much as 8 or 10 miles. Winds high up spread the top into a flat, anvil shape.

Updrafts move air away from the hot earth, and cold air from the top of the cloud falls rapidly toward the earth. Airplanes stay away from thunderheads because these up and down drafts could tear the airplane apart.

Inside the cloud there may be snow, ice, rain, or hail. Lightning flashes from top to bottom and from side to side.

What Causes Thunder?

It is certain that thunder is related to lightning. But the relationship is not clear. Several theories have been suggested to explain why there is thunder.

1. A lightning stroke creates a vacuum. The sound is produced when air rushes in to fill the vacuum.

2. Water drops in the atmosphere are turned into steam. As the steam expands, it produces the rumble of thunder.
3. Lightning breaks water molecules into hydrogen and oxygen. The two gases recombine explosively and produce the clap of thunder.
4. Lightning causes intense heating of the air along its path, just as electricity causes heating of a wire. Rapid expansion of the hot air causes thunder.

Each of these facts probably contributes to thunder. But the main influence is the last — heating followed by rapid expansion of the air.

Temperatures along the path of a lightning discharge may reach 30 000° Celsius, and the pressure may become 10 to 100 times greater than the normal pressure of the atmosphere. The air expands very rapidly, and part of the energy the gases contain is converted to the loudest of all natural sounds.

If you listen carefully you'll notice there may be loud cracks, rumbles, or booms depending on the nature of the lightning in the storm.

A lightning flash usually begins at the bottom of a cloud about five kilometers above the earth where the temperature is − 10° Celsius. This is the region where water droplets freeze. Electric charges build up there, sometimes reaching 300 million volts.

The flash begins when electrons released from the droplets collide with air, freeing more electrons. The charge of electrons may extend 50 to 100 meters. Another step begins, carrying the charge still further. Most usually this extension is still within the cloud, but also more toward the earth.

Sparks may be given off by tall objects on earth such as steeples or tall trees. When a spark reaches the step of lightning, a path to the ground is made. A discharge between earth and the cloud begins — the return stroke of lightning. The movement from the cloud to the ground may take a few thousandths of a second, but the return stroke is completed in just a few millionths. Movement to earth and back to the cloud may continue many times in a single flash, making the lightning stroke pulsate.

The steps of the flash may be only a few meters long, or as much as 100 meters. You can see the steps

in the jagged shape of the flash. Each step produces thunder. Loud, ear-splitting cracks occur when the sound waves of many steps reach you together. Rolling, sustained sound occurs when the sound of various steps not in a direct line to you reaches you at delayed intervals.

The lightning channel may be five kilometers long, and often it is much longer. Thunder lasts because sound from the nearest part of the channel reaches you before sound from the farthest part.

You can estimate the length of the channel from the length of time that the thunder lasts. Count the number of seconds that the thunder lasts and multiply that answer by one-third of a kilometer.

How Far Away Is the Storm?

Thunder is an air explosion. When you blow up a paper bag and then burst it you are making an air explosion. Multiply this effect millions of times and you have thunder. The lightning stroke heats air, pushes it out of the path, and sets the air to vibrating — producing sound. Since lightning and thunder occur at the same instant, you can find the distance to a storm by measuring the time it takes thunder to reach you.

Light travels 300 000 kilometers (186,000 miles) a second, so it reaches you almost the instant it is produced. Sound travels much more slowly — only 330 meters (1100 feet) a second.

As soon as you see the lightning, start counting seconds. (You can do this by saying, "one thousand one, one thousand two," and so on. Don't count fast; use a steady, comfortable speed.) Count until you hear the thunder. If there are three seconds between the flash and the thunder, the lightning occurred one kilometer away. If the time is five seconds, the storm is one mile away.

The Most Thunder and the Least Thunder

Each year the island of Java in Indonesia averages 322 days during which there are thunderstorms.

In the polar regions thunder and lightning storms are unknown because the towering thunderheads do not develop there.

Thunder curdles cream. Lightning sours milk.

Before there was refrigeration, farm people kept milk in cellars and springs. Lightning could not reach it there, it is true, but the real reason it was kept in such places was to keep it cool.

If cream curdled and milk soured, the reasons for it were not thunder and lightning. The souring was probably caused by the higher temperatures that often occur just before a thunderstorm.

Lightning Don'ts

Lightning kills more people than do tornadoes, hurricanes, and all other storms put together. When there's a lightning storm:

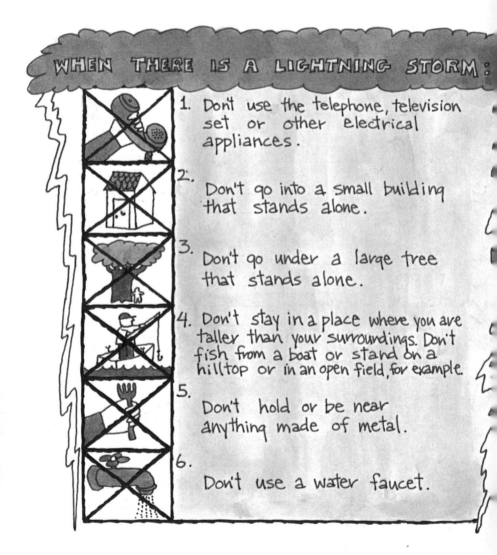

WHEN THERE IS A LIGHTNING STORM:

1. Don't use the telephone, television set or other electrical appliances.

2. Don't go into a small building that stands alone.

3. Don't go under a large tree that stands alone.

4. Don't stay in a place where you are taller than your surroundings. Don't fish from a boat or stand on a hilltop or in an open field, for example.

5. Don't hold or be near anything made of metal.

6. Don't use a water faucet.

5. Red Sky at Night — Clouds, Fog, Contrails, and Distrails

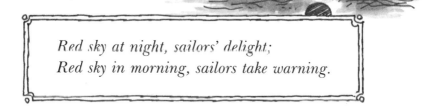

> *Red sky at night, sailors' delight;*
> *Red sky in morning, sailors take warning.*

Many of our weather beliefs began thousands of years ago. The Bible, in Matthew 16:2–3, says, "When it is evening, ye say, it will be fair weather: for the sky is red. And in the morning, It will be foul weather today, for the sky is red and lowering."

Is this a true saying? You can find out by keeping records of sky conditions and the weather that follows. If you don't get up early enough to see the sunrise, keep a record of sunsets and the weather on the following day.

61

At many locations good weather often follows a red sunset. This is because the weather generally comes from the west.

If the sunset is red, the air west of you must be quite dry and free from heavy clouds. As that air moves toward you it will bring fair weather.

When the sunrise is red, the clearer air is in the east. It moves away as the day progresses. Clouds may develop west of you and bring unsettled weather, probably rain or snow.

This may not be true where you live. At the eastern end of Long Island, red sunsets are usually followed by good weather, but a red sunrise is not always followed by a rainy day. The best way to find out what happens in your area is to keep a record of the weather and sky colors.

Shapes of Clouds

Clouds form when the sky temperature is a bit lower than that of the region directly beneath the cloud. When rising water vapor reaches the cooler region, it condenses into water droplets. If the temperature is below freezing, ice crystals form. Very high, thin and wispy clouds are made of these crystals.

Rainy-day clouds are produced by air that is rising over a wide area. The clouds contain tons of water, and they may extend over several hundred square kilometers.

During fair weather, puffs of clouds occur here and there. Small regions of the earth, such as plowed fields or paved parking areas, are warmer than their surroundings and hot air rises from them. As it rises, the air expands and cools. The water vapor condenses into droplets and forms a small tufted cloud.

FORMATION OF A THUNDER CLOUD

CROSS WINDS

HOT AIR

When a large volume of hot air rises, a thunder-head forms. The air rises so fast that the cloud stretches upward, sometimes towering several hundred kilometers. At the top of the cloud crosswinds may sweep the top sideways into the shape of an anvil. These and other isolated clouds are always changing shape because of the currents moving upward and the winds at higher elevations.

Sometimes the base of a formation of clouds is parallel to the horizon. The straight bottom edge marks the condensation level — that's where the temperature is cool enough for water vapor to condense. A large cumulus cloud (30 cubic miles) may contain 150,000 tons of water.

Forecasting Weather by Clouds and Winds

Thin, wispy clouds indicate fairly dry air, while heavy clouds result when air is laden with water droplets. So clouds are weather indicators. Winds blow from various directions because of temperature and pressure differences. So winds are also weather indicators. When the two are combined, they provide the basis for forecasts that are often quite accurate, especially in the northeastern part of the country. Use the chart below to make your own forecasts. You may find they are quite accurate.

SUMMER FORECAST

WIND DIRECTION ➡	N	E	S	W	
CLEAR (sky less than ¼ covered)	Fair, Cooler	Fair	Cloudier	Fair	
CIRRUS	Fair, Cool	Cloudier	Warm, showers	Fair	
ALTOCUMULUS	Showers	No change	showers	Fair	
ALTOSTRATUS	Fair, Cool	Cloudy	Clearing	Showers	
NIMBOSTRATUS	Improving	Improving	Improving	Improving	
CUMULUS	Cool, Rain	Showers	Rain, then Clear	Fair	
STRATOCUMULUS	Unsettled	No change	showers	No change	

CLOUD COVER

* IF CALM, USE WEST

WINTER FORECAST

	N	E	S	W	CLOUD COVER
	Fair, cooler	Cloudier	Cloudy, warm	Fair	CLEAR (sky less than ¼ covered)
	Unsettled	Unsettled	Warm, cloudy	No change	CIRRUS
	Warmer	Warmer	Warmer	Clear	ALTOCUMULUS
	Unsettled	Improving	Warm, clear	Clear, Cold	ALTOSTRATUS
	Cold	Stormy	Stormy	Colder	NIMBOSTRATUS
	Cool, clear	Showers	Rain, warm	Cold	CUMULUS
	Unsettled	Rain, warm	Rain, warm	Cold, clear	STRATOCUMULUS

Types of Clouds

There are dozens of different cloud forms. Each day they seem to change. However, the various clouds are combinations of the following three main types.

Cirrus (or curly): These are separate, and usually white, patches or bands. They have a filmy, hairlike appearance.

Cumulus (heap): These are usually a mound of clouds, towering upward from a flat base. They are sometimes called cauliflower clouds. Sunlit parts are brilliant white, while bases are darker.

Stratus (layer): These cover much of the sky and usually are connected or continuous and often gray and laden with rain or snow. The disk of the sun can often be seen through them. They often spread over large areas.

Combinations of these three basic cloud types produce a good many other forms of clouds. Some of
these are:

Cirrus

Cirrocumulus: Thin white sheets of clouds with grains
and ripples; quite regular in appearance.

Cirrostratus: Transparent, white veil of clouds; often
covering a large part of the sky.

Cumulus

Altocumulus: White or gray patches or sheets with
rounded mounds; may be separate or
merge together.

Cumulonimbus: Heavy, dense, high towers; top
often flattened into anvil shape — storm
clouds.

Stratocumulus: Usually lower than nimbostratus (see
below); gray or white rounded masses
that may merge or be separate.

Stratus

Altostratus: Gray sheet or layer that covers much of
the sky; here and there sunlight can be
seen through them.

Nimbostratus: Sometimes called nimbus cloud. Gray
cloud layer, often dark; produces rain
or snow, blots out the sun; ragged clouds
often form beneath the main clouds.

Jet Planes Make Clouds

High-flying airplanes release large amounts of water in the exhaust from their engines. At high altitudes, where temperatures are low, the vapor condenses immediately into water droplets. These produce the string of cloud that trails behind the plane. When there are large numbers of these *contrails* (condensation trails) they may blend together to make a sheet of cirrus clouds. If the air is very dry, the contrails evaporate quickly.

A *distrail* (dissipation trail) is a clear area that forms within a cloud. As a plane flies through the cloud, heat from the engine causes water droplets to evaporate and a clear trail is made through the cloud.

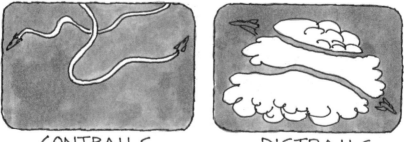

CONTRAILS   DISTRAILS

Weather scientists believe that contrails are changing the weather between Detroit and Des Moines. Every day some 700 jet planes fly through that area, which has been called the jet corridor.

In the midwest, since the jet age began, contrails that develop into high cirrus clouds have produced 53 per cent more cloudy days than there used to be. Over a long period these jet-produced clouds cause an increase in rain and snow and a cooling of summer temperatures in daytime and a warming at night. Chicago, which has the busiest airport in the world, is getting cooler, cloudier, and rainier, as are most of the places along the jet corridor.

Make a Cloud in a Bottle

When you breathe out on a cold day, you can see your breath. Warm air has a lot of water vapor in it. When your warm breath meets chilly air, the vapor it contains condenses — it changes to droplets. A cloud is formed. When you snap open a can or bottle of cold soda on a hot day, a cloud often forms and rapidly disappears. The cloud is close to the top of the can or in the neck of the bottle.

When you opened the cold soda can you released pressure on the contents. There was rapid expansion of the air above the soda. That caused cooling, so the vapor quickly condensed into droplets, forming a cloud.

You can make a cloud using a bottle, a bottle cap, and a pump.

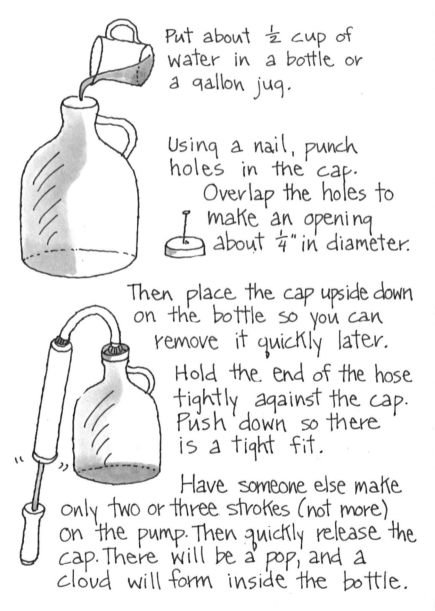

Put about ½ cup of water in a bottle or a gallon jug.

Using a nail, punch holes in the cap. Overlap the holes to make an opening about ¼" in diameter.

Then place the cap upside down on the bottle so you can remove it quickly later.

Hold the end of the hose tightly against the cap. Push down so there is a tight fit.

Have someone else make only two or three strokes (not more) on the pump. Then quickly release the cap. There will be a pop, and a cloud will form inside the bottle.

THIS IS WHY:

The air inside was pushed together by the pump; it was compressed. That made the air a little warmer, so it could hold a lot of water vapor. When you released pressure on the cap, the air spread out; it expanded. That made the air a little cooler. The cooler air could not hold as much vapor, so droplets formed. And that's what a cloud is — water droplets that are held in the air.

Particles in Clouds

The droplets in clouds are produced when vapor condenses on dust, ash, or particles of various salts suspended in the air. These are condensation nuclei.

Salt particles enter the air through the evaporation of ocean spray. Because of their small size, the salt particles are carried along in the air. Wind blowing over inland salt flats may also add salt particles. Particles of sulfur are released into the air when fuels are burned. Winds blowing over the desert pick up fine particles of sand and carry them to high altitudes. The sulfur salts, which come from car exhausts, make rainfall slightly acid. When these salts are present in larger amounts, acid rain is produced.

Dew, Frost, and Fog

In early mornings of spring and autumn the grass is often wet, or frosted if the temperature is below freezing. That's because during the night the ground loses heat by radiation. The air touching the ground will also be chilled. When the air is calm and it contains enough water vapor, some of the vapor condenses. Droplets collect on the grass and on cars and bikes left outside. If it's cold enough, the vapor changes into ice crystals.

If vapor condenses into droplets on particles in the lower air, such as tiny bits of salt, dust, or pollen grains, there will be a ground fog.

Fogs can be very dangerous and cause expensive delays in airplane flights. It is possible to clear fog away, but only at great expense, and then over only a small area and for a limited time.

The easiest way is to blow it away. This has been done at some airports, using giant fans. But in most places fog rolls in as fast as the fans can blow it away.

Warming the air is another way. But many burners are needed to produce enough heat to evaporate the water droplets, and fuel is costly. Also, this method may set up currents that produce conditions for making more fog.

Another way is to seed the fog with dry ice particles. When the temperature is low enough, the dry ice causes the droplets to change to ice crystals. These crystals then fall to earth or evaporate and change to invisible water vapor.

All methods of getting rid of fog are only partly successful. The best solution is not to produce the fog in the first place. Around airports where fog is a hazard, there should be no factories or power plants to send particles into the air, and airports should not be built near large bodies of water. People know this, but airports are still often built in places where fogs are likely to form.

Clear moon, frost soon.
or
Clear sky, frost nigh.

Earth cools by radiation, and when the sky is clear radiation is rapid. On cloudy nights, there is less chance of frost because the clouds act as blankets, preventing loss of heat from earth — the temperature on land stays above freezing.

6. Hurricanes, Tornadoes, and Dancing Devils

An old verse says, "When the wind is in the south, the rain is in its mouth. The wind in the west suits everyone best."

That's true for many locations, but some of the winds that come from the west don't suit people at all.

Hurricanes

Severe tropical storms are called hurricanes in the Atlantic and typhoons in the western Pacific in the China Sea. They may have winds more than 200 miles per hour. The screaming winds can uproot trees and blow houses apart. The storms usually originate near the equator. Air masses create strong vertical currents

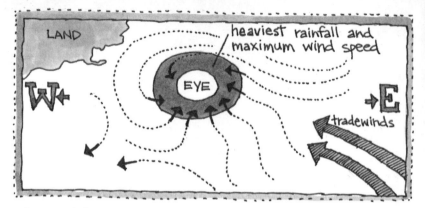

that swirl around, making a ring of clouds around a clear core — the eye of the hurricane. The entire mass of air moves westward. The clouds spread from the ring in a large pinwheel formation. Pressure drops rapidly toward the center of the storm. The barometer may fall two inches below the normal 30 inches of mercury.

At the center, or eye, which is an area 5 to 30 miles across, wind speeds drop to 10 to 15 miles an hour or less. Air sinks into the low-pressure "hole" and clouds there are broken, so the sun shines through. Around the edge of the eye, wind speeds increase from calm to maximum speed within a distance of only a few feet. Here the clouds seem thickest and rainfall the heaviest. This is the wall of the eye. As the storm moves farther west and north, the eye and the wall become less distinct; they tend to blend into the surrounding clouds.

As the eye approaches land, winds blow from the east; as it moves away, they blow from the west.

The entire storm mass moves north and westward, carried along by prevailing winds. As it nears land, the storm often swings farther north and then north-east. Its movements may become unpredictable. The strong winds produce a sea surge — a wall of water that may be twenty feet high or more. When it strikes land, the surge damages buildings, boats, piers, trees, houses, and beaches.

The storm mass is laden with hot air that cools as it rises, producing heavy rain. Eight to ten inches of rain may fall in a few hours. The flooding may be just as disastrous as the wind and the sea surge.

Hurricane Warning

Satellites keep watch on cloud formations to see if they are developing into the doughnut shape that is typical of a hurricane. When winds reach 39 miles per hour, the formation is called a tropical storm. If winds reach 74 miles per hour, the storm is called a hurricane.

Hurricane hunter planes fly into the hurricane to measure temperature, humidity, air pressure, and wind speed and direction. When weather watchers think the storm may reach land within 24 hours, they put out a hurricane warning.

People who live near the sea move inland before the storm can reach them. Sometimes, roads are flooded and it becomes impossible to move. If a house is on high land that won't be flooded, people may remain there, but there are safety rules to be followed.

Hurricane Safety Rules

1. Store clean water in the bathtub, and in jugs and bottles. City water may be cut off or become unfit for drinking.

2. Board up large windows. Crisscross smaller windows with tape to prevent flying glass.

3. Pick up loose things in the yard. Toys, tools, flower pots, and sticks become like bullets when picked up by the wind.

4. Stay indoors. Don't go out to save something you may have overlooked. The wind could blow you down. You might be hit by flying debris or a falling tree.

5. Beware the eye of the hurricane. The wind may stop, and the sky may clear, but the hurricane is not over. Soon the wind will blow again; this time from the opposite direction as the storm passes by.

6. Have a battery-powered radio so you can hear news about the hurricane if the electric power is cut off.

7. Have a flashlight with fresh batteries.

Some Notable Hurricanes

Hurricanes used to be given female names, the first of the season beginning with *A*, the second with *B*, and so on. Today, both male and female names are used in the same *A, B, C* order.

Arlene: August 2, 1963. Gusts reached 97 miles per hour at Bermuda, off the east coast of the United States. The eye was 28 miles wide.

Inez: September 24, 1966. Winds up to 197 miles per hour. Changed path suddenly and entered the Gulf of Mexico.

Camille: August 17, 1969. Most destructive in modern times along the Gulf coast and east coast of the United States. Winds reached 200 miles per hour and tides surged 24 feet; 300 people were lost and there was a billion dollars of damage. In Virginia 27 inches of rain fell in 24 hours.

Inga: September 20, 1969. Winds up to 90 miles per hour moved in an erratic path through the mid-Atlantic region. Lasted 25 days as a severe storm.

Ginger: September 4 to October 5, 1971 off the east coast. Longest severe storm. During its 31 days there were 20 days of hurricane-strength winds. Eye was very large — about 80 miles across. Storm often reversed itself.

Gloria: September 29, 1985. Winds of 100 miles per hour swept along the east coast. Crossed Long Island and into New England. Widespread damage from the wind, though there was very little rain in most locations.

Hurricane Ditty

June, too soon;
July, stand by;
August, look out!
September, you will remember;
October, all over.

Tornadoes

Every year tornadoes cause severe damage and kill many people. They are associated with the dark cumulonimbus clouds produced when warm, moist air moving north meets cool, dry air coming from the west. A funnel-shaped cloud tapers down from a wide part of the cloud to form a narrow tip. If it reaches the ground it can cause damage, but sometimes the tip remains harmlessly above ground. The tip may bob up and down, skipping over one town and causing devastation in another. The funnel may be pushed sideways by the wind. Several funnels may extend from a single dark storm cloud formation. When the storm develops over water, the funnel formation is called a water spout.

Inside the funnel, winds spiral around and upwards at speeds of 200 to 300 miles per hour. The funnel moves along the ground much more slowly; usually at speeds of 20 to 30 miles per hour. Inside the funnel air pressure is very low. The drop is so steep and sudden that when a tornado approaches a building, the air inside, which remains at high pressure, may push outward with so much force that the building explodes. This is why people open windows as a tornado approaches — so the inside pressure will equal the outside pressure.

Ways That Tornadoes Cause Damage

Wind force: The wind blows so fast, it exerts tremendous force — more than enough to knock down buildings and turn over cars and trucks.

Twist force: Wind speed at the edge of a tornado is uneven. A building at the edge of a tornado may be twisted out of the ground because the wind is so much stronger on one side of it than on the other.

Explosive force: Pressure inside the funnel is much less than pressure outside of it. When a funnel approaches a building, the air inside the building can cause it to explode.

Lift and drop: Because of the low pressure and high winds in the funnel, people, cars, trucks, trees, loose boards, and other debris are pushed into the funnel. The funnel sucks them into the air where they are carried along and may be dropped and destroyed. People may be killed. Or, they may be set down softly without any injury.

Tornado Safety Rules

AT HOME

1. Open the windows a little, then get away from them.

2. Go to a storm cellar if you have one.

3. If you don't have a storm cellar, get under a heavy workbench in the cellar, under a staircase, or under a mattress or heavy blanket.

4. Don't stay inside a mobile home; go to a strong building or a storm cellar.

1. Get off the street.

2. Go into a building but keep away from windows and doors.

3. If you are not near a building, lie flat in a ditch and cover your head.

4. In school, go to an inside hall on the lowest floor; bend over with your hands on the back of your head.

5. In school, keep away from big rooms such as gyms, cafeterias, and auditoriums.

BROOM CLOSET

A Tornado Scale

Some tornadoes are more powerful than others. To measure them Professor T. Theodore Fujita of Chicago has made this scale:

1. Very Weak: winds up to 110 kilometers per hour (72 mph); snaps off TV antennas.
2. Weak: winds up to 180 kilometers per hour (112 mph); overturns house trailers.
3. Strong: winds up to 225 kilometers per hour (157 mph); tears roofs off houses, blows cars off roads.
4. Severe: winds up to 320 kilometers per hour (206 mph); uproots trees, blows down walls of buildings.
5. Devastating: winds up to 410 kilometers per hour (260 mph); flattens buildings — causes great destruction.
6. Incredible: winds up to 500 kilometers per hour (318 mph).

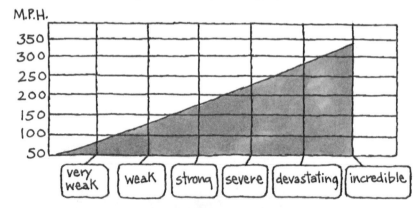

Since 1916 the United States has had almost 25,000 tornadoes. Twenty thousand of these were rated 1, 2, or 3. There were 127 tornadoes scaled at number 6.

Wind: Breath from the Earth

Down through history there have been various explanations of the winds. Aristotle, the Greek scientist and philosopher, explained winds by saying that earth breathed both hot and cold. His idea of a breathing earth persisted for hundreds of years. As late as the seventeenth century many people believed that sea breezes blew steadily and always in the same direction because they came from the "constant breath" of a single kind of plant — the seaweed that extended over a large part of the ocean. They believed that land breezes were more apt to blow in various directions and with uneven force because they were the breath of a wide variety of plants.

Air Moves

You can't see air move, and often you can't feel it move, but air moves just about all the time. Movements of large amounts of air cause changes in the weather. Usually air masses move across the United States from the west toward the east. Air moves because it is at different temperatures. All air is pulled down by gravity, but cold air is pulled down more than warm air. The cooler air digs under the warmer air and pushes it up and out of the way.

Try this to "see" air move. You'll need a soda straw, a pin, a paper clip, a piece of Styrofoam, a small cereal box, some glue, and cardboard. Pinch the ends of the straw. Fasten the paper clip to one end. Staple or glue a piece of light cardboard (about 2 by 2 inches) to the other end.

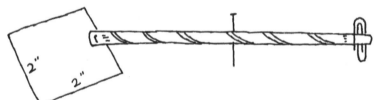

1. Put a pin through the center of the straw. Be sure the straw moves easily around the pin.

2. Glue a small piece of styrofoam to a small cereal box. Then put the pin into the styrofoam. If the straw doesn't balance, move the paper clip until it does. If it still doesn't balance, add another paper clip. You have made an air current detector.

3. Hold it over a lamp. Air currents will make the detector move if the box is not too big.

Put the detector on a table. Hold a tray of ice cubes over it. Then put the ice cubes under it. Hold the detector over a radiator or near the floor in front of an open refrigerator. You'll discover that there are air currents in your house — movements of air you don't usually notice.

You can also make an air spinner that turns whenever there are movements of air. You'll need a pencil, an empty spool or a wad of clay, a needle, some cardboard, and the top to a ballpoint pen.

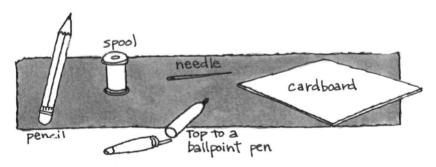

To make your spinner, cut out the spiral as shown below.

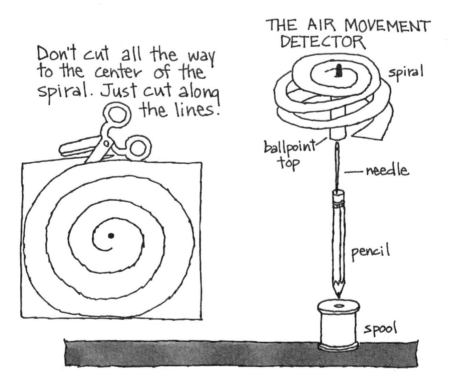

Don't cut all the way to the center of the spiral. Just cut along the lines!

THE AIR MOVEMENT DETECTOR

spiral

ballpoint top

needle

pencil

spool

Put the plastic ballpoint top through a hole cut in the center of the spiral. If there's a clip on the plastic top, cut it off carefully. Push a needle into the eraser of the pencil. Then put the cap over the end of the needle. The spool (or wad of clay) makes a stand for your spinner. Put the spinner on a radiator or hold it over a lamp or stand it near a window or on a table.

A Storm in a Cake Pan

Convection is motion between liquids or gases of different temperatures. It is largely responsible for winds and violent storms. You can see how convection works by using a glass pan and a few drops of food coloring.

Fill the pan with water and place one end of it over a small burner. Turn the burner on as low as possible. Add a drop or two of food coloring at the cool end of the pan. Look at the pan from the side and watch the action of the colored water. It will move down and toward the warm end; then rise upward and back to the cool end. This is a convection current. It is much the same as the convection currents in the atmosphere.

The liquid moves because of unbalanced pressure. The density of the cool water is greater than that of the warm water. The cool water tends to sink and the liquid at the top moves toward the cooler area. This increases pressure at the cold side, and decreases pressure at the warm side. The liquid at the bottom is pushed toward the warm side.

Movements between air masses at different temperatures occur in the same way. So your model is a good illustration of what happens in the atmosphere.

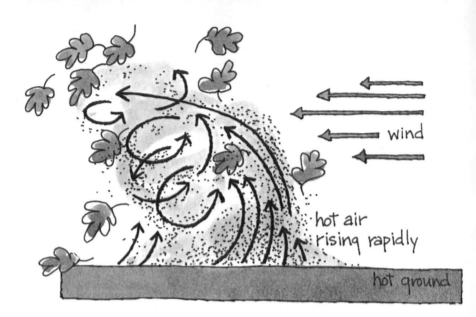

wind

hot air rising rapidly

hot ground

Dancing Devils

Perhaps you have seen leaves in a field or bits of paper in a large parking lot whirling upwards. The leaves and paper are lifted by a small upward-moving flow of air. The land is heated and so is the air touching it — this hot air rises rapidly. As it does so, the air spins around and it picks up loose material. In a desert, the air carries sand; these are called dust devils, sand devils, or simply dancing devils. A person might see a dozen or so at the same time.

The sand may be carried 300 feet high or, rarely, even much higher. Most devils last only a few moments. If they continue to swirl, they may develop considerably in size and height. Dust devils can then become dangerous — somewhat like a small tornado.

Santa Ana — The Witch's Wind

Once every year, and sometimes more often, a northeast wind blows through the Santa Ana Canyon towards Los Angeles, and southward from Santa Barbara to Mexico. It is called the Santa Ana, or Witch's Wind, because of the damage it causes. Sixty times in this century the wind has spread disastrous fires throughout the area. It is a hot, drying wind that makes tinder out of fields and forests. In 1970 a fire started in a landfill and sparks were blown for miles. Before it ended, eight days later, the fire had stretched over 150 miles. Fourteen people died from smoke and fire. A thousand homes were burned to the ground. Half a million acres were burned out, leaving nothing but ashes.

Usually this area is cooled by a sea breeze from the Pacific. But occasionally the breeze stops and the pressure drops. Meanwhile a high-pressure mass from Canada stalls in the region to the west. It picks up heat and blows toward the sea — high pressure air blowing toward low pressure. The Santa Ana is born, temperatures go up fast, and the hot moving air dries up fields and forests.

Similar winds blow in other parts of the world. They are called *foehns*, hot, dry occasional winds. In Austria and Switzerland foehns ("ferns") often reach 80 miles an hour. They cause flash floods as they melt the snow. People get aches and pains during the foehn season; they get edgy and uncomfortable because rapid changes in pressure and humidity affect blood circulation and the nervous system. Probably some people also worry about the damage the winds may cause.

In the Rockies the foehn is so warm it may melt and evaporate as much as two feet of snow in 24 hours. Because of this, the wind is called a *chinook* — the Indian word for snow-eater.

Horse Latitudes

In the area 30 degrees north and south of the equator there is a region of calm seas that is called the *horse latitudes*. In the days of sailing ships, ships blown into this region would often be becalmed for weeks. No one is sure where the name comes from, but some of these ships carried horses as cargo, and there is a legend that tells of one skipper who harnessed the horses to his ship and put them overboard to pull it out of the calms.

Samuel Taylor Coleridge, the English poet, described the horse latitudes in "The Rime of the Ancient Mariner."

> *Day after day, day after day,*
> *We stuck, nor breath nor motion;*
> *As idle as a painted ship*
> *Upon a painted ocean.*

Winds Around the World

Different parts of the world have their own names for particular winds that blow in the region. Here are a few of them:

NAME	LOCATION	REMARKS
BALI	JAVA	STRONG, EASTERLY
BLIZZARD	U.S., CANADA	COLD, NORTHERLY
BURGA	ALASKA	SNOW, SLEET
CHILI	MEDITERRANEAN	HOT, SPRING, SOUTH
CHINOOK	U.S.	DRY, WARM
COCKEYED BOB	AUSTRALIA	SQUALLS, STORMS
ELEPHANTA	INDIA	SOUTHEASTERLY
KHAMSIN	EGYPT	EASTERLY, HOT SAND
LEVANTER	GIBRALTAR	STRONG, EASTERLY
MISTRAL	MEDITERRANEAN	COLD, DRY, NORTHERLY
PURGA	SIBERIA	COLD, VIOLENT, SNOW
SIMMOOM	MEDITERRANEAN	HOT, DRY, DUSTY
SIROCCO	MEDITERRANEAN	WARM, DAMP, SOUTHERLY
STEPPINWIND	GERMANY	COLD, NORTHEASTERLY
WILLIWAW	ALASKA	SUDDEN SQUALL
ZONDA	ARGENTINA	HOT, DRY, WESTERLY

Wind Direction Indicator

An arrow that is free to swing around a bearing makes a good wind vane.

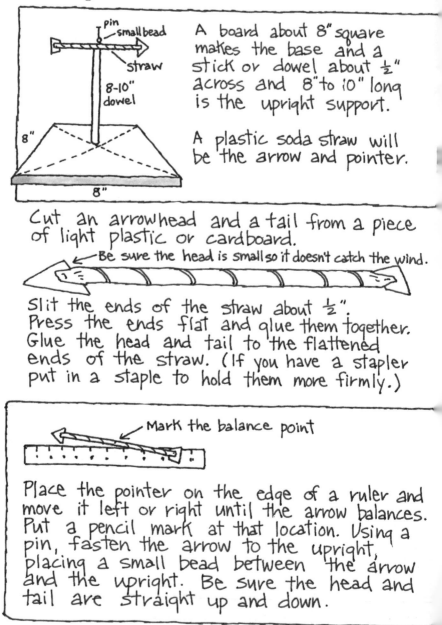

A board about 8" square makes the base and a stick or dowel about ½" across and 8" to 10" long is the upright support.

A plastic soda straw will be the arrow and pointer.

Cut an arrowhead and a tail from a piece of light plastic or cardboard.

Be sure the head is small so it doesn't catch the wind.

Slit the ends of the straw about ½". Press the ends flat and glue them together. Glue the head and tail to the flattened ends of the straw. (If you have a stapler put in a staple to hold them more firmly.)

Mark the balance point

Place the pointer on the edge of a ruler and move it left or right until the arrow balances. Put a pencil mark at that location. Using a pin, fasten the arrow to the upright, placing a small bead between the arrow and the upright. Be sure the head and tail are straight up and down.

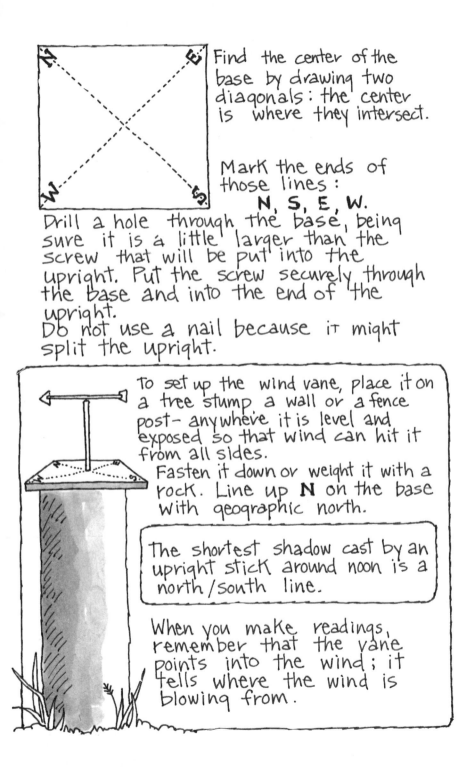

Find the center of the base by drawing two diagonals: the center is where they intersect.

Mark the ends of those lines:
N, S, E, W.

Drill a hole through the base, being sure it is a little larger than the screw that will be put into the upright. Put the screw securely through the base and into the end of the upright.

Do not use a nail because it might split the upright.

To set up the wind vane, place it on a tree stump a wall or a fence post — anywhere it is level and exposed so that wind can hit it from all sides.

Fasten it down or weight it with a rock. Line up **N** on the base with geographic north.

The shortest shadow cast by an upright stick around noon is a north/south line.

When you make readings, remember that the vane points into the wind; it tells where the wind is blowing from.

Measuring Wind Speed

You can make a device to indicate wind speed using a milk carton, pins, and a soda straw.

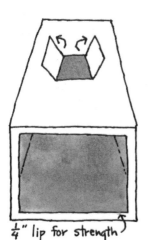

$\frac{1}{4}$" lip for strength

1" long slit

cardboard

1. Cut out both ends of a milk carton, leaving about $\frac{1}{4}$" around the edge. Then make a cut along the center of the carton and also about 1" toward each side. Bend up the two flaps. These will support the movable pointer and leave a hole in the center of the carton.

2. To make the pointer cut an inch-long slit in one end of a plastic soda straw. Flatten the end and glue it together.

3. Cut a square piece of cardboard so it fits easily cross-wise inside the milk carton. Glue or staple this flapper to the flattened end of the soda straw.

4. Put the pointer inside the carton, straw end first so the straw comes up through the opening in the carton. Put a long pin through a tab of the carton and then through the straw and through the other tab. Be sure the straw is straight up and down.
If you blow into the carton, the flapper will move and so will the straw.

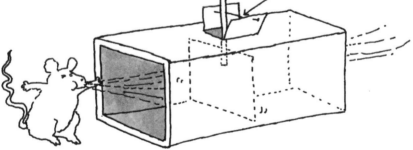

To use the indicator you will need a scale showing wind speeds. Glue a piece of cardboard to a side of the carton. It must be a fairly large piece as shown in the drawing.

Face the indicator into the wind, so the wind moves the flapper. Using a marking pen, mark wind speeds on the cardboard scale. You can find wind speeds by using the scale on page 103. Notice what is happening to trees, leaves, flags, etc. If they indicate a wind speed of 12 miles per hour, let us say, write the number at the location of the pointer. After a while you'll have a scale of wind speeds on the cardboard scale. Then, whenever you want to measure wind speed, place your indicator so the wind blows into it and you'll be able to read wind speed from the position of the pointer. (You may have to fasten down the indicator with a couple of thumb tacks so it doesn't blow away.)

WIND SCALE

		M.P.H.
	smoke rises	0
	smoke drifts	1-3
	Leaves rustle; flags stir	4-7
	Leaves and twigs move	8-12
	Branches move; flags flap	13-18
	Small trees sway; flags ripple	19-24
	Large branches move; flags beat	25-31
	Whole trees move; flags extend	32-38
	Twigs break; walking is difficult	39-46
	Signs, antennas blow down	47-54
	Trees uprooted; damage to buildings	55-73
	Countryside devastated	74+ hurricane

tropical storms

A cow with its tail to the west,
makes weather the best;
A cow with its tail to the east,
makes weather the least.

Watch cows in a field and you'll notice that they all tend to face in the same direction. They keep their heads out of the wind, probably because it's more comfortable for them that way.

When the cows' tails are to the west, there is a west wind. And this is most often a fair-weather wind.

When their tails are toward the east, there is an east wind; one that very often brings stormy weather.

Bibliography

Branley, Franklyn M. *Dinosaurs, Asteroids and Super-stars*. New York: Crowell, 1982.

Cohen, Daniel. *What's Happening to Our Weather*. New York: Evans, 1979.

Forrester, Frank H. *1001 Questions Answered about the Weather*. New York: Dover, 1984.

Holford, Ingrid. *Guinness Weather Facts and Feats*. New York: Sterling, 1977.

Iger, Eve Marie. *Weather on the Move*. Reading, Mass.: Addison Wesley, 1970.

Kals, W. S. *The Riddle of the Winds*. New York: Doubleday, 1977.

Kaufmann, John. *Winds and Weather*. New York: Morrow, 1971.

Ludlum, David M. *The American Weather Book.* Boston: Houghton Mifflin, 1982.

Sattler, Helen R. *Nature's Weather Forecasters.* Nashville, Tenn.: Nelson, 1978.

Sloane, Eric. *Weather Lore.* New York: Duell, Sloan and Pearce, 1963.

Index

111